Paul Cadmus

90 YEARS OF DRAWING

Essay by Justin Spring

D C **MOORE**

GALLERY

724 FIFTH AVENUE

NEW YORK NY 10019

TEL 212 247 2111

FAX 212 247 2119

Paul Cadmus: Drawing from the Heart

"To draw does not mean simply to reproduce contours; drawing does not consist of merely lines; drawing is also expressive, the inner form . . ."   —Ingres

THIS EXHIBITION, a celebration of ninety years of drawing by Paul Cadmus, is surprisingly enough the first Cadmus exhibition ever to be devoted exclusively to his drawings. At a time when few galleries mount full-scale drawing shows, this one seems particularly important, for Cadmus' extraordinarily expressive draughtsmanship lies at the very heart of his work, the very center of his art.

Taken individually, each of the works in this show is an object of beauty, and the most beautiful of them are among the most accomplished drawings of the twentieth century. Together, however, they are something more, for they demonstrate the gradual evolution of an artist over the course of nine decades—and, not coincidentally, picture a number of the most important people in Paul Cadmus' life. For Cadmus, drawing has always been a deeply personal act; not surprisingly, the best of his drawings are frequently of family, friends and lovers.

Cadmus was born to artist parents in New York in December, 1904. Both his father, who had studied under Robert Henri, and his mother, who worked as a magazine illustrator, encouraged Paul and

Woman, 1909
Crayon on paper
8⅛ × 6½ inches

his sister Fidelma in their artistic inclinations. As a result, a number of Cadmus' earliest drawings have been preserved, including one of a woman (completed at age 4) which Cadmus jokingly refers to as being "from my de Kooning period." Several later pen-and-ink sketches of Fidelma demonstrate Cadmus' precocious talent (as well as his affection for his sister). Another picture, one depicting an ocean liner, was created in the same year the Titanic met its doom. These early works demonstrate the close, natural, early relationship that Cadmus had with drawing. Their joy and ease carry no suggestion of the very difficult circumstances in which the Cadmus family lived. But it is important to note that poverty left its mark: during his boyhood, Cadmus suffered from rickets, a disease brought on by malnutrition, which may account, to some extent, for his lifelong appreciation of good health, fitness and physical beauty.

Cadmus left school at fifteen to study art at the National Academy of Design. At the age of sixteen, he earned a bronze medal at the Academy for his proficiency in drawing. He was naturally gifted and hard-working. "I admire discipline, and have admired it since I was a young man," he told me recently. "[But my own discipline] didn't come to me from my father, or from art school. I just had it."

By the time he left the academy in 1926 (after six years of coursework) Cadmus had won many prizes and scholarships. From 1923 to

Hinky Dinky Parley Voo, 1939
Pen, ink, and wash on paper
7 inches in diameter

1931 he exhibited his work and occasionally published illustrations in the book review section of the *New York Herald Tribune*. From 1928 to 1931 he worked in an advertising agency. But his style was never much influenced by commercial illustration, for he did little of that sort of work; his job with the advertising agency consisted primarily of designing and laying out pages.

In 1931, Cadmus' artistic career began in earnest when the painter Jared French, convinced Cadmus to quit his well-paid job in advertising, use his savings to travel to Europe, and, as Cadmus recalls, "be an artist." Their first stop was Paris. From there, they proceeded to Chartres, where they bought bicycles and toured down through France and Spain.

Drawing was Cadmus' foremost preoccupation. He recalls that "one of the first [things I did] in Europe [in] October 1931 was to go to Montauban, because it's Ingres home town, and that's where the Ingres Museum is, and that's where the largest selection of works by Ingres were located." Ingres, civilized and sensual, was always his hero, much more so than even Rembrandt. According to Cadmus, the next most important influence on him was Luca Signorelli, whose work he had long known in reproduction. Signorelli's incisive and highly sculptural frescoes, which Cadmus observed in the cathedral at Orvieto, made a deep and lasting impression. While some might assume that Cadmus' early and abiding interest in the descriptive quality of line developed out of his printmaking experiences in the 1920s, Cadmus knows otherwise: "That interest in line, and awareness of its descriptive abilities—that really came from looking at Signorelli." Other highly important influences from Cadmus' European period include Piero della Francesca (who would also be a great inspiration to Jared French), and Matthias Grünewald (Cadmus' favorite northern

Snow Fences, 1944
Ink and pencil on paper
10 5/16 × 8 5/8 inches

European painter, particularly for his Isenheim Altarpiece at Colmar).
He also admired the later artists Degas and Seurat.

When not travelling across Europe to museums and historical sites,
Cadmus and French lived a relaxed and pleasurable life in Puerto de
Andraitx, Mallorca, where Cadmus created a number of substantial
drawings and paintings, including the now-famous *Y.M.C.A. Locker
Room*, *Shore Leave* and *Bicyclists* (all from 1933). These paintings,
and the many which followed, show Cadmus' ongoing preoccupation
with figuration (particularly the male body) and, of course, with
line. It is worth noting that throughout his more ambitious oils and
watercolors of the period, Cadmus returns again and again to line,
using it to define form and volume in a highly tactile and sensual
manner. Drawings made by Cadmus during his Mallorcan period in
this show include *Jared French* (1932) and *Cuddy* (1932).

In 1933, his savings spent, Cadmus returned to New York and
enrolled in the Public Works of Art Project. When his 1934 painting
The Fleet's In! was ejected from an exhibition at the Corcoran Gallery
for its depiction of lecherous drunken sailors, the scandal gave Cadmus
instant notoriety and prompted a new phase of his career. The often
grotesque, sexually-charged satirical images which followed drew
upon art-historical precedents (most particularly the genre and alle-
gorical scenes of the Northern European Old Masters) but had an
all-American, street-smart feeling to them as well. These works were
often developed through preliminary drawings, such as the two for
Wild Party (1939). At the same time, however, Cadmus continued to
make less controversial works which show a continued interest in the
expressive and quietly sensual qualities of line, such as the powerful
portrait of his future brother-in-law, *Lincoln Kirstein* (1937) and the
study of his artist friend *Ilse Bischoff* (1939).

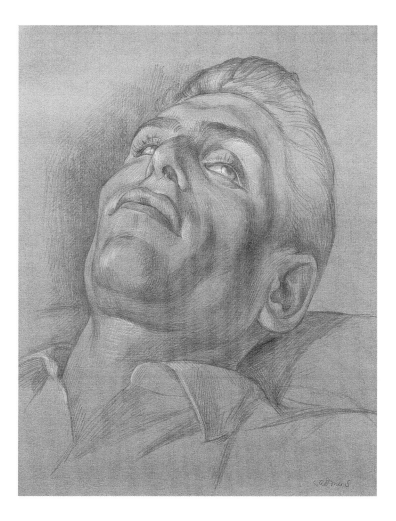

Enzo no. 2, c. 1951
Pencil and white watercolor on gray paper
9¼ × 8⅜ inches

During the 1940s, Cadmus' drawings continued to include preparatory works for paintings; they also increasingly featured finished nudes, both male and female, suggesting that, while social satire still interested him, the artist was entering a quieter, more sensual, less histrionic phase. *Male Nude B17* (c. 1940) and *Nina* (c. 1945) give a good sense of Cadmus' renewed interest in Ingres-inspired depictions of the human form. But Cadmus' life has always been a social one, and other drawings from the period depict images outside the studio. The study for the painting *Conversation Piece* (1940) gives us his good friends Monroe Wheeler, novelist Glenway Wescott, and photographer George Platt Lynes lounging in various stages of undress beneath a willow tree at "Stone Blossom," the New Jersey farmhouse where Cadmus was a frequent guest of Wheeler and Wescott. Cadmus has always enjoyed drawing his friends and lovers; his portrait drawings from this period include the painter *George Tooker* (1949), as well as his friend *Bridget Bate Chisholm* (ca. 1945). And there have always, of course, been self-portraits. Cadmus' fascinating *Self Portrait* (1948) becomes particularly interesting when viewed alongside *Self Portrait 1.22.98* (1998), an equally expressive drawing of fifty years later.

In the early 1940s, Cadmus increasingly created drawings as finished works of art, working with hand toned papers, colored crayons, chalk, silverpoint and casein as a way of enriching and adding depth to his work. Even so, he has never subscribed to the Victorian idea of the sketch as one of the highest forms of art (in that it provides greater insight into the creative process than any other). Nor does he subscribe to the idea of drawing as an act of exploration or self-expression, an idea he associates with the abstract expressionist movement. "I don't like that sort of work," he says firmly. "Art of that sort, the art of self-expression, seems to me to go directly to the canvas without craft."

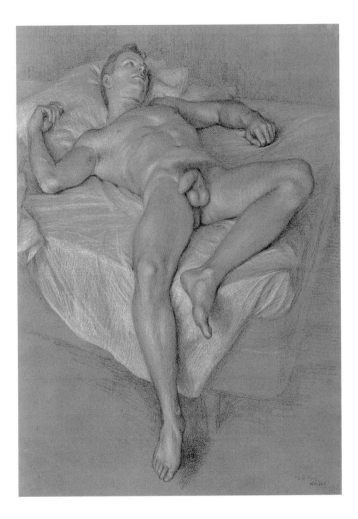

Male Nude NM126, 1965–66
Crayons on paper
23 × 17 inches

Study for David and Goliath, 1964
Crayons on gray Strathmore paper
11¼ × 13½ inches

Kneeling Figure NM97, 1972
Crayon on hand-toned paper
14½ × 10½ inches

(The only expressionists Cadmus has ever admired, he says, were the German expressionists Otto Dix and George Grosz.) Still, he says, "I do prefer some artist's drawings to their paintings—Fuseli, for instance. And I do think a sketch can have more vitality than a finished work."

Cadmus has no hard-and-fast way of creating a drawing, for he creates many sorts of drawings, and inevitably varies his methods to suit his ends. "Drawings for paintings are one thing, drawings for drawings are another." he says. "I often do a preparatory drawing for a finished drawing. I do a preliminary sketch just to make sure I've got everything as I like it. Then I transfer the outline [which is often on tracing paper] to a prepared paper."

During the 1950s, many Cadmus paintings, including *The Bath* (1951) and *Finistère* (1952), show an open preoccupation with available male sexuality and male beauty, particularly the beauty of young men. At a time when homosexuality was deemed criminal, these works tested the boundaries of accepted taste, and indeed, in our own age, many still do. But Cadmus has never been much involved in what is now known as gay rights activism, nor has he ever wanted to create drawings or paintings of sexual acts. (He did once create a series of about two dozen drawings, based on a photographic album lent to him by Allen Porter of the Museum of Modern Art, which are now in the collection of the Kinsey Institute, but he did so only for his own pleasure, and with no expectation of developing them into saleable or finished works.) "I've never thought of [my drawings or paintings] as political acts," Cadmus told me recently. "And I never think of them as aiming to add to public consciousness, but maybe they have. In certain cases—particularly in reproduction in books, I think—they help people who are far from cultural climates

The Venetian Chair NM170, 1983
Crayons on toned Strathmore paper
21 × 16¾ inches

like New York ... people in Ohio and such. It helps them feel they are not alone."

In Cadmus' drawings of the male nude, a distance always seems to exist between the artist and his beautiful subjects, as if to suggest that the encounter is made more satisfying by distance and restraint. His nude and portrait drawings of the 1950s are mostly of men, notably the model Teodor Starkowski. Other 1950s drawings in this show include still-life studies for paintings: *Sock Dryer and Towel*, a preparatory drawing for *The Bath* (1951), and *Sketch for Bar Italia no. G1* (1954), a preparatory drawing for the raucously satiric painting of the same name (1953–55).

Throughout the late 1950s and early 60s, Cadmus continued to draw and paint the male nude. In 1965 he met Jon Anderson, the man who would become his muse, model, life partner, and (not coincidentally) the subject of some of his most beautiful drawings. These grand, classically inspired works (most in colored chalk and crayon on hand-toned paper) have an atmosphere of intent, relaxed sensuality worthy of Prud'hon or Ingres. The series, which number over 270, are called the "NM" series (not, as some have thought, meaning "Nude Man," but rather "Nantucket Man," for Cadmus met Anderson on Nantucket, and it was there that the series began.)

From 1965 to the present, Cadmus has continued to explore all aspects of the male nude, relying mostly upon Anderson as his model (he has now embarked upon a "Z" series); the work he has created with Anderson combines a reserved but blissful eroticism with virtuosic formal explorations (specifically of torsion and foreshortening), and innovative, often witty composition. Remarkably, Anderson remains nearly as handsome and physically prepossessing today as he was thirty years ago; Cadmus has been lucky indeed in his choice of a model.

Study for *Shame!*, 1991–92
Pencil, pen and ink, and crayons on tracing paper
24 × 11⅛ inches

When I asked Cadmus recently how his own age has affected his perception of physical beauty, he thought for a moment, then replied, "I don't know. Sometimes I'm ashamed that I'm so interested in physical beauty, but I am. I like looking at beautiful people." Asked about the physical challenge of age, he responded, "I don't know what you mean by physical challenges, unless you mean laziness. *That's* a challenge!"

It is Paul Cadmus' way to deflect questions about his work with disarmingly simple answers, and to insist, as well, that his work is merely one aspect of his busy and richly varied life. On a recent visit to his studio, for example, I listened, amused and somewhat skeptical, as this urbane, congenial, and dazzlingly well-read 93-year-old man insisted that "the word industrious has never applied to me. I'm basically lazy."

His work told me otherwise. Drawing, that seemingly most simple of artistic acts, is in fact the most demanding. To draw as Cadmus does requires years of discipline, years of training, years of paying close and constant attention to the complex visual experience most of us, particularly in an age of photographic reproduction, take almost entirely for granted. Cadmus' seemingly effortless drawings (whatever their politics, whatever their subjects) represent nothing less than a ninety-year engagement in the art and craft of drawing.

"I feel that in trying to draw beauty that exists in nature, nature always wins—that I can never actually catch the beauty," He said at the conclusion of my visit to his studio, as he was about to return to work on a drawing of Jon Anderson. "But I can keep trying. And I do."

—Justin Spring

This catalogue was published on the
occasion of the exhibition held at
DC Moore Gallery, 724 Fifth Avenue
at 57th Street in New York, from
May 5 through June 19, 1998.

Paul Cadmus
is exclusively represented by
D C Moore Gallery

Design: Marcus Ratliff
Composition: Amy Pyle
Photography: Kevin Ryan
Imagesetting: Center Page
Lithography: V & L Printers